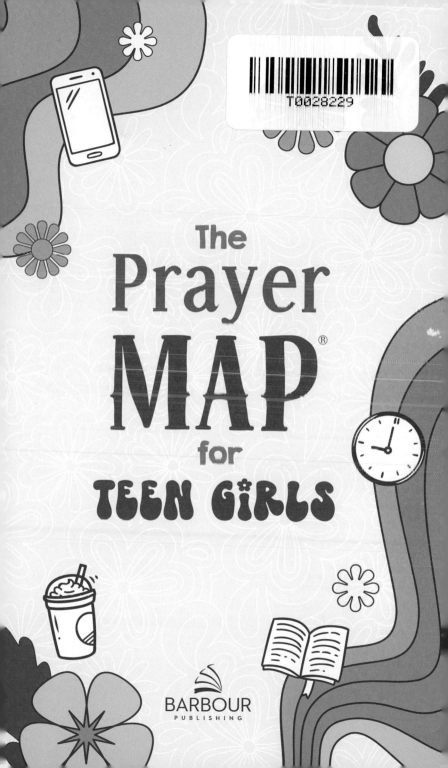

The Prayer MAP®
for
TEEN GIRLS

BARBOUR
PUBLISHING

Published by Barbour Publishing, Inc., 1810 Barbour Drive, Uhrichsville, Ohio 44683, www.barbourbooks.com

Our mission is to inspire the world with the life-changing message of the Bible.

Member of the
Evangelical Christian
Publishers Association

Printed in China.

What does prayer look like?

What kinds of things should I pray about?

Do my prayers matter to God?

And does He really hear every word I pray?

Discover the power of prayer with this colorful and creative prayer journal that guides you to create your very own prayer map—as you write out specific thoughts, ideas, and lists, which you can follow (from start to finish!)—as you talk to God. (Be sure to write the date on each one of your prayer maps so you can look back over time and see how God is working in your life!)

The Prayer Map for Teen Girls will not only encourage you to spend time talking with God about the things that matter most (to you and to Him!). . .it will also help you make daily prayer a habit—for life!

Date:

DEAR GOD, ...
....
....
....

I'm thankful for. . . ..
....
....
....
....
....
....
....
....
....

People I am praying for. . .
....
....
....
....
....

My worries. . .
....
....
....
....
....
....
....
....
....
....
....
....
....
....

Here's what's going on in my life. . . ..
....
....
....
....
....
....

My needs. . .

....
....
....
....
....
....
....
....
....
....
....
....

**Other stuff I need
to share with You, God. . .**

....
....
....
....
....
....
....

AMEN.

*Thank You, God,
for hearing my prayers!*

*"O Lord, please hear my prayer!
Listen to the prayers of those of us
who delight in honoring you."*

NEHEMIAH 1:11

Date:

DEAR GOD,

....
....
....
....

I'm thankful for. . . ..
....
....
....
....
....
....
....
....
....

People I am praying for. . .
....
....
....
....
....

My worries. . .
....
....
....
....
....
....
....
....
....
....
....
....
....

Here's what's going on in my life. . .

....
....
....
....
....
....

My needs. . .

....
....
....
....
....
....
....
....
....
....
....

Other stuff I need to share with You, God. . .

....
....
....
....
....
....

AMEN.

Thank You, God, for hearing my prayers!

The earnest prayer of a righteous person has great power and produces wonderful results.

JAMES 5:16

Date:

DEAR GOD,

....
....
....
....

I'm thankful for. . .

....
....
....
....
....
....
....
....

People I am praying for. . .

....
....
....
....
....

My worries. . .

....
....
....
....
....
....
....
....
....
....
....
....
....

Here's what's going on in my life. . .

....

....

....

....

....

My needs. . .

....

....

....

....

....

....

....

....

....

....

....

....

Other stuff I need to share with You, God. . .

....

....

....

....

....

....

AMEN.

Thank You, God, for hearing my prayers!

Listen to my cry for help, my King and my God, for I pray to no one but you.
PSALM 5:2

Date:

DEAR GOD,

....
....
....
....

I'm thankful for. . . ..
....
....
....
....
....
....
....
....

People I am praying for. . .
....
....
....
....
....

My worries. . .

....
....
....
....
....
....
....
....
....
....
....
....
....
....

Here's what's going on in my life. . .

....
....
....
....
....
....

My needs. . .

....
....
....
....
....
....
....
....
....
....
....

Other stuff I need to share with You, God. . .

....
....
....
....
....
....
....

AMEN.
Thank You, God, for hearing my prayers!

Pray that the Lord's message will spread rapidly and be honored wherever it goes.
2 THESSALONIANS 3:1

Date:

DEAR GOD, ...
....
....
....

I'm thankful for. . . ..
....
....
....
....
....
....
....
....

My worries. . .
....
....
....
....
....
....
....
....
....
....
....
....
....
....

People I am praying for. . .
....
....
....
....
....

Here's what's going on in my life. . .

....
....
....
....
....
....
....

My needs. . .

....
....
....
....
....
....
....
....
....
....
....

Other stuff I need to share with You, God. . .

....
....
....
....
....
....
....

AMEN.
Thank You, God, for hearing my prayers!

"Keep on asking, and you will receive what you ask for. Keep on seeking, and you will find. Keep on knocking, and the door will be opened to you."

MATTHEW 7:7

Date:

DEAR GOD,

....
....
....
....

I'm thankful for. . . ..
....
....
....
....
....
....
....
....

People I am praying for. . .
....
....
....
....
....

My worries. . .
....
....
....
....
....
....
....
....
....
....
....
....
....
....

Here's what's going on in my life. . . ..

....

....

....

....

....

....

My needs. . .

....

....

....

....

....

....

....

....

....

....

....

**Other stuff I need
to share with You, God. . .**

....

....

....

....

....

....

....

AMEN.

*Thank You, God,
for hearing my prayers!*

*Hear me as I pray, O LORD.
Be merciful and answer me!*
PSALM 27:7

Date:

DEAR GOD,

....

....

....

....

I'm thankful for. . . ..

....

....

....

....

....

....

....

....

People I am praying for. . .

....

....

....

....

....

My worries. . .

....

....

....

....

....

....

....

....

....

....

....

....

....

....

Here's what's going on in my life. . .

....
....
....
....
....

My needs. . .

....
....
....
....
....
....
....
....
....
....

Other stuff I need to share with You, God. . .

....
....
....
....
....
....

AMEN.

Thank You, God, for hearing my prayers!

Devote yourselves to prayer with an alert mind and a thankful heart.
COLOSSIANS 4:2

Date:

DEAR GOD,

....
....
....
....

I'm thankful for. . . ..
....
....
....
....
....
....
....
....

People I am praying for. . .
....
....
....
....
....
....

My worries. . .
....
....
....
....
....
....
....
....
....
....
....
....
....

Here's what's going on in my life. . .

....

....

....

....

....

My needs. . .

....

....

....

....

....

....

....

....

....

....

....

Other stuff I need to share with You, God. . .

....

....

....

....

....

....

AMEN.

Thank You, God, for hearing my prayers!

"O Lord, you are a great and awesome God! You always fulfill your covenant and keep your promises of unfailing love to those who love you and obey your commands."

DANIEL 9:4

Date:

DEAR GOD, ...
....
....
....

I'm thankful for. . . ..
....
....
....
....
....
....
....
....
....

People I am praying for. . .
....
....
....
....
....
....

My worries. . .
....
....
....
....
....
....
....
....
....
....
....
....
....
....

Here's what's going on in my life. . .

....

....

....

....

....

....

My needs. . .

....

....

....

....

....

....

....

....

....

....

....

Other stuff I need to share with You, God. . .

....

....

....

....

....

....

....

AMEN.
Thank You, God, for hearing my prayers!

But each day the LORD pours his unfailing love upon me, and through each night I sing his songs, praying to God who gives me life.

PSALM 42:8

Date:

DEAR GOD, ...
....
....
....

I'm thankful for. . . ..
....
....
....
....
....
....
....
....

My worries. . .
....
....
....
....
....
....
....
....
....
....
....
....
....
....

People I am praying for. . .
....
....
....
....
....
....

Here's what's going on in my life. . .

....

....

....

....

....

....

My needs. . .

....

....

....

....

....

....

....

....

....

....

....

Other stuff I need to share with You, God. . .

AMEN.

Thank You, God, for hearing my prayers!

I pray that God, the source of hope, will fill you completely with joy and peace because you trust in him.

ROMANS 15:13

Date:

DEAR GOD, ...
....
....
....

I'm thankful for. . . ..
....
....
....
....
....
....
....
....

My worries. . .
....
....
....
....
....
....
....
....
....
....
....
....
....

People I am praying for. . .
....
....
....
....
....

Here's what's going on in my life. . .

....

....

....

....

....

....

My needs. . .

....

....

....

....

....

....

....

....

....

....

....

Other stuff I need to share with You, God. . .

....

....

....

....

....

....

AMEN.

Thank You, God, for hearing my prayers!

"Pray with all your might! And don't let up!"
1 SAMUEL 7:8 MSG

Date:

DEAR GOD,

....
....
....
....

I'm thankful for. . . ..
....
....
....
....
....
....
....
....

People I am praying for. . .
....
....
....
....
....
....

My worries. . .
....
....
....
....
....
....
....
....
....
....
....
....
....

Here's what's going on in my life. . .

....
....
....
....
....
....

My needs. . .

....
....
....
....
....
....
....
....
....
....
....
....

Other stuff I need to share with You, God. . .

....
....
....
....
....
....
....

AMEN.
Thank You, God, for hearing my prayers!

We always pray for you, and we give thanks to God, the Father of our Lord Jesus Christ.
Colossians 1:3

Date:

DEAR GOD,

....
....
....
....

I'm thankful for. . .

....
....
....
....
....
....
....
....
....
....

My worries. . .

....
....
....
....
....
....
....
....
....
....
....
....
....

People I am praying for. . .

....
....
....
....
....
....

Here's what's going on in my life. . . ..
....
....
....
....
....

My needs. . .

....
....
....
....
....
....
....
....
....
....
....
....

**Other stuff I need
to share with You, God. . .**

....
....
....
....
....
....
....

AMEN.
*Thank You, God,
for hearing my prayers!*

*Pray for all people. Ask God to
help them; intercede on their behalf,
and give thanks for them.*
1 TIMOTHY 2:1

Date:

DEAR GOD, ...
....
....
....

I'm thankful for. . . ..
....
....
....
....
....
....
....
....

People I am praying for. . .
....
....
....
....
....
....

My worries. . .
....
....
....
....
....
....
....
....
....
....
....
....
....

Here's what's going on in my life. . .

....

....

....

....

....

....

My needs. . .

....

....

....

....

....

....

....

....

....

....

....

....

Other stuff I need to share with You, God. . .

....

....

....

....

....

....

AMEN.

*Thank You, God,
for hearing my prayers!*

*Answer my prayers, O Lord,
for your unfailing love is wonderful.*
PSALM 69:16

Date: _____

DEAR GOD, ...
....
....
....

I'm thankful for. . . ..
....
....
....
....
....
....
....
....
....

My worries. . .
....
....
....
....
....
....
....
....
....
....
....
....

People I am praying for. . .
....
....
....
....
....

Here's what's going on in my life. . .

My needs. . .

Other stuff I need to share with You, God. . .

AMEN.

Thank You, God, for hearing my prayers!

They will pray for you with deep affection because of the overflowing grace God has given to you.

2 CORINTHIANS 9:14

Date:

DEAR GOD,

....
....
....
....

I'm thankful for. . . ..
....
....
....
....
....
....
....
....

My worries. . .
....
....
....
....
....
....
....
....
....
....
....
....
....

People I am praying for. . .
....
....
....
....
....

Here's what's going on in my life. . .

....

....

....

....

....

....

My needs. . .

....

....

....

....

....

....

....

....

....

....

....

Other stuff I need to share with You, God. . .

....

....

....

....

....

....

....

AMEN.
Thank You, God, for hearing my prayers!

Because he bends down to listen, I will pray as long as I have breath!
PSALM 116:2

Date:

DEAR GOD, ...
....
....
....

I'm thankful for. . . ..
....
....
....
....
....
....
....
....

My worries. . .
....
....
....
....
....
....
....
....
....
....
....
....
....
....

People I am praying for. . .
....
....
....
....
....

Here's what's going on in my life. . .

....
....
....
....
....
....

My needs. . .

....
....
....
....
....
....
....
....
....
....
....
....

Other stuff I need to share with You, God. . .

....
....
....
....
....
....
....

AMEN.

Thank You, God, for hearing my prayers!

I pray that from his glorious, unlimited resources he will empower you with inner strength through his Spirit.

EPHESIANS 3:16

Date:

DEAR GOD,

....
....
....
....

I'm thankful for. . . ..
....
....
....
....
....
....
....
....

People I am praying for. . .
....
....
....
....
....
....

My worries. . .

....
....
....
....
....
....
....
....
....
....
....
....
....

Here's what's going on in my life. . .

....
....
....
....
....
....

My needs. . .

....
....
....
....
....
....
....
....
....
....
....
....

Other stuff I need to share with You, God. . .

....
....
....
....
....
....
....

AMEN.

Thank You, God, for hearing my prayers!

GOD, O God of Israel, there is no God like you in the skies above or on the earth below, who unswervingly keeps covenant with his servants and unfailingly loves them while they sincerely live in obedience to your way.

2 CHRONICLES 6:14 MSG

Date:

DEAR GOD, ...
....
....
....

I'm thankful for. . . ..
....
....
....
....
....
....
....
....
....

My worries. . .
....
....
....
....
....
....
....
....
....
....
....
....
....

People I am praying for. . .
....
....
....
....
....
....

Here's what's going on in my life. . . ..
....
....
....
....
....

My needs. . .

....
....
....
....
....
....
....
....
....
....
....
....

Other stuff I need to share with You, God. . .

....
....
....
....
....
....
....

AMEN.

Thank You, God, for hearing my prayers!

God's way of putting people right shows up in the acts of faith, confirming what Scripture has said all along: "The person in right standing before God by trusting him really lives."

ROMANS 1:17 MSG

Date:

DEAR GOD, ...
....
....
....

I'm thankful for. . . ..
....
....
....
....
....
....
....
....

My worries. . .
....
....
....
....
....
....
....
....
....
....
....
....
....

People I am praying for. . .
....
....
....
....
....

Here's what's going on in my life. . . ..
....
....
....
....
....

My needs. . .

....
....
....
....
....
....
....
....
....
....
....

**Other stuff I need
to share with You, God. . .**

....
....
....
....
....
....
....

AMEN.

*Thank You, God,
for hearing my prayers!*

*I lift my hands to you in prayer. I thirst
for you as parched land thirsts for rain.*

PSALM 143:6

Date:

DEAR GOD,
....
....
....
....

I'm thankful for. . . ..
....
....
....
....
....
....
....
....

People I am praying for. . .
....
....
....
....
....

My worries. . .
....
....
....
....
....
....
....
....
....
....
....
....
....
....

Here's what's going on in my life. . .

....
....
....
....
....
....

My needs. . .

....
....
....
....
....
....
....
....
....
....
....
....

Other stuff I need to share with You, God. . .

....
....
....
....
....
....

AMEN.

Thank You, God, for hearing my prayers!

"Bless those who curse you. Pray for those who hurt you."
LUKE 6:28

Date:

DEAR GOD,

....
....
....
....

I'm thankful for. . . ..
....
....
....
....
....
....
....
....
....

People I am praying for. . .
....
....
....
....
....

My worries. . .
....
....
....
....
....
....
....
....
....
....
....
....
....
....
....

Here's what's going on in my life. . .

....
....
....
....
....
....

My needs. . .

....
....
....
....
....
....
....
....
....
....
....
....

Other stuff I need to share with You, God. . .

....
....
....
....
....
....
....
....

AMEN.

Thank You, God, for hearing my prayers!

I pray that your love will overflow more and more, and that you will keep on growing in knowledge and understanding.

PHILIPPIANS 1:9

Date:

DEAR GOD,

....
....
....
....

I'm thankful for. . . ..
....
....
....
....
....
....
....
....
....

People I am praying for. . .
....
....
....
....
....

My worries. . .

....
....
....
....
....
....
....
....
....
....
....
....
....
....

Here's what's going on in my life. . . ..
....
....
....
....
....
....

My needs. . .

....
....
....
....

....
....
....
....
....
....
....

**Other stuff I need
to share with You, God. . .**

....
....
....
....
....
....

AMEN.

*Thank You, God,
for hearing my prayers!*

*"Love your enemies! Pray for
those who persecute you!"*

MATTHEW 5:44

Date:

DEAR GOD,

....
....
....
....

I'm thankful for. . . ..
....

My worries. . .
....
....
....
....
....
....
....
....
....
....
....
....
....
....
....

People I am praying for. . .
....
....
....
....
....

Here's what's going on in my life. . . ..
....
....
....
....
....
....

My needs. . .

....
....
....
....
....
....
....
....
....
....
....

Other stuff I need to share with You, God. . .

....
....
....
....
....
....

AMEN.

Thank You, God, for hearing my prayers!

I'm thanking you, God, out loud in the streets, singing your praises in town and country. The deeper your love, the higher it goes; every cloud is a flag to your faithfulness.

PSALM 57:9–10 MSG

Date:

DEAR GOD, ...
....
....
....

I'm thankful for. . . ..
....
....
....
....
....
....
....
....

My worries. . .
....
....
....
....
....
....
....
....
....
....
....
....
....

People I am praying for. . .
....
....
....
....
....
....

Here's what's going on in my life. . . ..

....

....

....

....

....

....

My needs. . .

....

....

....

....

....

....

....

....

....

....

....

....

**Other stuff I need
to share with You, God. . .**

....

....

....

....

....

....

....

AMEN.

*Thank You, God,
for hearing my prayers!*

I pray to you, O LORD, my rock.
PSALM 28:1

Date:

DEAR GOD, ...
....
....
....

I'm thankful for. . . ..
....
....
....
....
....
....
....
....

People I am praying for. . .
....
....
....
....
....

My worries. . .
....
....
....
....
....
....
....
....
....
....
....
....
....

Here's what's going on in my life. . .

....
....
....
....
....
....

My needs. . .

....
....
....
....
....
....
....
....
....
....
....
....

Other stuff I need to share with You, God. . .

....
....
....
....
....
....
....

AMEN.

Thank You, God, for hearing my prayers!

I also pray that you will understand the incredible greatness of God's power for us who believe him.

EPHESIANS 1:19

Date:

DEAR GOD,

....
....
....
....

I'm thankful for. . . ..

....
....
....
....
....
....
....
....

My worries. . .

....
....
....
....
....
....
....
....
....
....
....
....
....

People I am praying for. . .

....
....
....
....
....

Here's what's going on in my life. . . ..
....
....
....
....
....

My needs. . .

....
....
....
....
....
....
....
....
....
....
....
....

**Other stuff I need
to share with You, God. . .**

AMEN.

*Thank You, God,
for hearing my prayers!*

*"You can pray for anything, and if
you have faith, you will receive it."*
MATTHEW 21:22

Date:

DEAR GOD,

....
....
....
....

I'm thankful for. . . ..
....
....
....
....
....
....
....
....

People I am praying for. . .
....
....
....
....
....

My worries. . .
....
....
....
....
....
....
....
....
....
....
....
....
....

Here's what's going on in my life. . .

....
....
....
....
....
....

My needs. . .

....
....
....
....
....
....
....
....
....
....
....

Other stuff I need to share with You, God. . .

....
....
....
....
....
....

AMEN.

Thank You, God, for hearing my prayers!

In your unfailing love, O God, answer my prayer with your sure salvation.

PSALM 69:13

Date:

DEAR GOD,

....
....
....
....

I'm thankful for. . . ..
....
....
....
....
....
....
....
....
....

My worries. . .
....
....
....
....
....
....
....
....
....
....
....

People I am praying for. . .
....
....
....
....
....

Here's what's going on in my life. . .

....

....

....

....

....

....

My needs. . .

....

....

....

....

....

....

....

....

....

....

....

....

Other stuff I need to share with You, God. . .

....

....

....

....

....

....

....

AMEN.

Thank You, God, for hearing my prayers!

God, I'm telling the world what you do!

PSALM 73:28 MSG

Date:

DEAR GOD, ...
....
....
....

I'm thankful for. . . ..
....
....
....
....
....
....
....

My worries. . .
....
....
....
....
....
....
....
....
....
....
....
....
....
....

People I am praying for. . .
....
....
....
....
....

Here's what's going on in my life. . .

....

....

....

....

....

....

My needs. . .

....

....

....

....

....

....

....

....

....

....

....

....

Other stuff I need to share with You, God. . .

....

....

....

....

....

....

....

AMEN.
Thank You, God, for hearing my prayers!

Jesus often withdrew to the wilderness for prayer.
LUKE 5:16

Date:

DEAR GOD, ...
....
....
....

I'm thankful for. . . ..
....
....
....
....
....
....
....
....
....

People I am praying for. . .
....
....
....
....
....
....

My worries. . .
....
....
....
....
....
....
....
....
....
....
....
....
....

Here's what's going on in my life. . . ..

....

....

....

....

....

My needs. . .

....

....

....

....

....

....

....

....

....

....

....

....

**Other stuff I need
to share with You, God. . .**

....

....

....

....

....

....

AMEN.

*Thank You, God,
for hearing my prayers!*

*Your love, GOD, is my song, and I'll sing it!. . .
I'll never quit telling the story of your love.*

PSALM 89:1 MSG

Date:

DEAR GOD, ...
....
....
....

I'm thankful for. . . ..
....
....
....
....
....
....
....
....

My worries. . .
....
....
....
....
....
....
....
....
....
....
....
....
....
....

People I am praying for. . .
....
....
....
....
....
....

Here's what's going on in my life. . .

....

....

....

....

....

....

My needs. . .

....

....

....

....

....

....

....

....

....

....

....

Other stuff I need to share with You, God. . .

....

....

....

....

....

....

....

AMEN.

Thank You, God, for hearing my prayers!

Praise God, who did not ignore my prayer or withdraw his unfailing love from me.

PSALM 66:20

Date:

DEAR GOD, ...
....
....
....

I'm thankful for. . . ....
....
....
....
....
....
....
....
....

My worries. . .
....
....
....
....
....
....
....
....
....
....
....
....
....
....

People I am praying for. . .
....
....
....
....
....
....

Here's what's going on in my life. . .

....
....
....
....
....
....

My needs. . .

....
....
....
....
....
....
....
....
....
....
....
....

Other stuff I need to share with You, God. . .

....
....
....
....
....
....
....

AMEN.

Thank You, God, for hearing my prayers!

The Holy Spirit prays for us with groanings that cannot be expressed in words.

ROMANS 8:26

Date:

DEAR GOD, ...
....
....
....

I'm thankful for. . . ..
....
....
....
....
....
....
....
....

People I am praying for. . .
....
....
....
....
....

My worries. . .
....
....
....
....
....
....
....
....
....
....
....
....
....

Here's what's going on in my life. . .

....
....
....
....
....
....

My needs. . .

....
....
....
....
....
....
....
....
....
....
....
....

Other stuff I need to share with You, God. . .

....
....
....
....
....
....

AMEN.

Thank You, God, for hearing my prayers!

Rejoice in our confident hope. Be patient in trouble, and keep on praying.

ROMANS 12:12

Date:

DEAR GOD, ...
....
....
....

I'm thankful for. . . ..
....
....
....
....
....
....
....
....

People I am praying for. . .
....
....
....
....

My worries. . .
....
....
....
....
....
....
....
....
....
....
....
....
....

Here's what's going on in my life. . . ..

....

....

....

....

....

....

My needs. . .

....

....

....

....

....

....

....

....

....

....

....

Other stuff I need to share with You, God. . .

....

....

....

....

....

....

....

....

AMEN.

Thank You, God, for hearing my prayers!

I can't keep quiet about you. GOD, my God, I can't thank you enough.
PSALM 30:12 MSG

Date:

DEAR GOD,

....
....
....
....

I'm thankful for. . . ..
....
....
....
....
....
....
....
....
....

People I am praying for. . .
....
....
....
....
....
....

My worries. . .
....
....
....
....
....
....
....
....
....
....
....
....
....

Here's what's going on in my life. . .

....
....
....
....
....
....

My needs. . .

....
....
....
....
....
....
....
....
....
....
....
....

**Other stuff I need
to share with You, God. . .**

....
....
....
....
....
....

AMEN.
*Thank You, God,
for hearing my prayers!*

*I am praying to you because I
know you will answer, O God.
Bend down and listen as I pray.*

PSALM 17:6

Date: ....

DEAR GOD, ...

....

....

....

I'm thankful for. . . ..

....

....

....

....

....

....

....

....

People I am praying for. . .

....

....

....

....

....

My worries. . .

....

....

....

....

....

....

....

....

....

....

....

....

....

Here's what's going on in my life. . .

....

....

....

....

....

....

My needs. . .

....

....

....

....

....

....

....

....

....

....

....

....

Other stuff I need to share with You, God. . .

....

....

....

....

....

....

....

....

AMEN.

Thank You, God, for hearing my prayers!

And you are helping us by praying for us.
2 CORINTHIANS 1:11

Date:

DEAR GOD, ...
....
....
....

I'm thankful for. . . ..
....
....
....
....
....
....
....
....

People I am praying for. . .
....
....
....
....
....

My worries. . .
....
....
....
....
....
....
....
....
....
....
....
....
....

Here's what's going on in my life. . .

....
....
....
....
....
....

My needs. . .

....
....
....
....
....
....
....
....
....
....
....
....

Other stuff I need to share with You, God. . .

....
....
....
....
....
....
....

AMEN.

Thank You, God, for hearing my prayers!

I love the LORD because he hears my voice and my prayer for mercy.

PSALM 116:1

Date:

DEAR GOD,
....
....
....
....

I'm thankful for. . . ..
....
....
....
....
....
....
....
....

My worries. . .
....
....
....
....
....
....
....
....
....
....
....
....
....

People I am praying for. . .
....
....
....
....
....

Here's what's going on in my life. . .

....
....
....
....
....

My needs. . .

....
....
....
....
....
....
....
....
....
....
....

Other stuff I need to share with You, God. . .

....
....
....
....
....
....

AMEN.

Thank You, God, for hearing my prayers!

I have not stopped thanking God for you. I pray for you constantly.
EPHESIANS 1:16

Date:

DEAR GOD, ...
....
....
....

I'm thankful for. . . ..
....
....
....
....
....
....
....
....

People I am praying for. . .
....
....
....
....
....

My worries. . .
....
....
....
....
....
....
....
....
....
....
....
....
....
....

Here's what's going on in my life. . .

....

....

....

....

....

My needs. . .

....

....

....

....

....

....

....

....

....

....

....

....

Other stuff I need to share with You, God. . .

....

....

....

....

....

AMEN.
Thank You, God, for hearing my prayers!

The LORD is my strength and shield. I trust him with all my heart. He helps me, and my heart is filled with joy. I burst out in songs of thanksgiving.

PSALM 28:7

Date:

DEAR GOD,

....
....
....
....

I'm thankful for. . .

....
....
....
....
....
....
....
....
....

People I am praying for. . .

....
....
....
....
....
....

My worries. . .

....
....
....
....
....
....
....
....
....
....
....
....
....

Here's what's going on in my life. . .

....
....
....
....
....
....

My needs. . .

....
....
....
....
....
....
....
....
....
....
....
....

Other stuff I need to share with You, God. . .

....
....
....
....
....
....

AMEN.
Thank You, God, for hearing my prayers!

I will praise you forever, O God, for what you have done. I will trust in your good name.

PSALM 52:9

Date:

DEAR GOD, ...
....
....
....

I'm thankful for. . . ..
....
....
....
....
....
....
....
....

My worries. . .
....
....
....
....
....
....
....
....
....
....
....
....
....

People I am praying for. . .
....
....
....
....
....

Here's what's going on in my life. . .

....
....
....
....
....
....

My needs. . .

....
....
....
....
....
....
....
....
....
....
....
....

Other stuff I need to share with You, God. . .

....
....
....
....
....
....

AMEN.

*Thank You, God,
for hearing my prayers!*

*You faithfully answer our prayers with
awesome deeds, O God our savior.
You are the hope of everyone on earth,
even those who sail on distant seas.*

PSALM 65:5

Date:

DEAR GOD, ...
....
....
....

I'm thankful for. . . ..
....
....
....
....
....
....
....
....
....

People I am praying for. . .
....
....
....
....
....

My worries. . .
....
....
....
....
....
....
....
....
....
....
....
....
....
....

Here's what's going on in my life. . .

....

....

....

....

....

My needs. . .

....

....

....

....

....

....

....

....

....

....

....

....

Other stuff I need to share with You, God. . .

....

....

....

....

....

....

AMEN.

Thank You, God, for hearing my prayers!

Pray in the Spirit at all times and on every occasion. Stay alert and be persistent in your prayers for all believers everywhere.

EPHESIANS 6:18

Date:

DEAR GOD,

....
....
....
....

I'm thankful for. . . ..
....
....
....
....
....
....
....
....

People I am praying for. . .
....
....
....
....
....

My worries. . .
....
....
....
....
....
....
....
....
....
....
....
....
....

Here's what's going on in my life...

....
....
....
....
....
....

My needs...

....
....
....
....
....
....
....
....
....
....
....

Other stuff I need to share with You, God...

....
....
....
....
....
....
....

AMEN.
Thank You, God, for hearing my prayers!

O LORD of Heaven's Armies, what joy for those who trust in you.
PSALM 84:12

Date:

DEAR GOD,

....
....
....
....

I'm thankful for. . .

....
....
....
....
....
....
....
....
....

People I am praying for. . .

....
....
....
....
....

My worries. . .

....
....
....
....
....
....
....
....
....
....
....
....
....

Here's what's going on in my life. . . ..
....
....
....
....
....
....

My needs. . .
....
....
....
....
....
....
....
....
....
....
....

**Other stuff I need
to share with You, God. . .**
....
....
....
....
....
....
....

AMEN.
*Thank You, God,
for hearing my prayers!*

*Whenever I pray,
I make my requests. . .with joy.*
PHILIPPIANS 1:4

Date:

DEAR GOD,

....
....
....
....

I'm thankful for. . . ..
....
....
....
....
....
....
....
....

People I am praying for. . .
....
....
....
....
....
....

My worries. . .

....
....
....
....
....
....
....
....
....
....
....
....
....

Here's what's going on in my life. . .

....
....
....
....
....
....

My needs. . .

....
....
....
....
....
....
....
....
....
....
....
....

Other stuff I need to share with You, God. . .

....
....
....
....
....
....
....

AMEN.
Thank You, God, for hearing my prayers!

"When you are praying, first forgive anyone you are holding a grudge against, so that your Father in heaven will forgive your sins, too."

MARK 11:25

Date:

DEAR GOD,

....
....
....
....

I'm thankful for. . .
....
....
....
....
....
....
....
....
....

People I am praying for. . .
....
....
....
....
....
....

My worries. . .
....
....
....
....
....
....
....
....
....
....
....
....

Here's what's going on in my life. . .

My needs. . .

Other stuff I need to share with You, God. . .

AMEN.

Thank You, God,
for hearing my prayers!

Don't worry about anything; instead, pray
about everything. Tell God what you need,
and thank him for all he has done.

PHILIPPIANS 4:6

Date:

DEAR GOD,

....
....
....
....

I'm thankful for. . . ..
....
....
....
....
....
....
....
....

People I am praying for. . .
....
....
....
....
....
....

My worries. . .

....
....
....
....
....
....
....
....
....
....
....
....
....

Here's what's going on in my life. . .

My needs. . .

Other stuff I need to share with You, God. . .

AMEN.

*Thank You, God,
for hearing my prayers!*

*I am praying that you will put into action
the generosity that comes from your faith
as you understand and experience all
the good things we have in Christ.*

PHILEMON 1:6

Date:

DEAR GOD,

....
....
....
....

I'm thankful for. . . ..
....
....
....
....
....
....
....
....

People I am praying for. . .
....
....
....
....
....

My worries. . .

....
....
....
....
....
....
....
....
....
....
....
....
....

Here's what's going on in my life. . .

....
....
....
....
....
....

My needs. . .

....
....
....
....
....
....
....
....
....
....
....
....

Other stuff I need to share with You, God. . .

....
....
....
....
....
....

AMEN.

Thank You, God, for hearing my prayers!

We have not stopped praying for you since we first heard about you. We ask God to give you complete knowledge of his will and to give you spiritual wisdom and understanding.

COLOSSIANS 1:9

Date:

DEAR GOD,

....
....
....
....

I'm thankful for. . . ..
....
....
....
....
....
....
....
....

My worries. . .

....
....
....
....
....
....
....
....
....
....
....
....
....

People I am praying for. . .
....
....
....
....
....

Here's what's going on in my life. . .

....

....

....

....

....

....

My needs. . .

....

....

....

....

....

....

....

....

....

....

....

Other stuff I need to share with You, God. . .

....

....

....

....

....

....

....

....

AMEN.

Thank You, God,
for hearing my prayers!

I will praise you as long as I live,
lifting up my hands to you in prayer.

PSALM 63:4

Date:

DEAR GOD, ...
....
....
....

I'm thankful for. . . ..
....
....
....
....
....
....
....
....

People I am praying for. . .
....
....
....
....
....

My worries. . .
....
....
....
....
....
....
....
....
....
....
....
....

Here's what's going on in my life. . .

....

....

....

....

....

....

My needs. . .

....

....

....

....

....

....

....

....

....

....

....

....

Other stuff I need to share with You, God. . .

....

....

....

....

....

....

....

AMEN.

Thank You, God, for hearing my prayers!

"Pray like this: Our Father in heaven, may your name be kept holy."
MATTHEW 6:9

Date:

DEAR GOD, ...
....
....
....

I'm thankful for. . . ..
....
....
....
....
....
....
....
....

People I am praying for. . .
....
....
....
....
....

My worries. . .
....
....
....
....
....
....
....
....
....
....
....
....
....
....
....

Here's what's going on in my life. . .

....
....
....
....
....
....
....

My needs. . .

....
....
....
....
....
....
....
....
....
....
....
....

Other stuff I need to share with You, God. . .

....
....
....
....
....
....

AMEN.

Thank You, God, for hearing my prayers!

We keep on praying for you, asking our God to enable you to live a life worthy of his call.

2 THESSALONIANS 1:11

Date:

DEAR GOD,

....
....
....
....

I'm thankful for. . . ..
....
....
....
....
....
....
....
....
....

People I am praying for. . .
....
....
....
....
....

My worries. . .

....
....
....
....
....
....
....
....
....
....
....
....
....

Here's what's going on in my life. . .

....
....
....
....
....
....

My needs. . .

....
....
....
....
....
....
....
....
....
....
....
....

Other stuff I need to share with You, God. . .

....
....
....
....
....
....
....

AMEN.
Thank You, God, for hearing my prayers!

As soon as I pray, you answer me; you encourage me by giving me strength.
PSALM 138:3

Date:

DEAR GOD, ...
....
....
....

I'm thankful for. . . ..

....
....
....
....
....
....
....
....

People I am praying for. . .

....
....
....
....
....

My worries. . .

....
....
....
....
....
....
....
....
....
....
....
....
....
....
....

Here's what's going on in my life. . . ..

....

....

....

....

....

My needs. . .

....

....

....

....

....

....

....

....

....

....

....

**Other stuff I need
to share with You, God. . .**

....

....

....

....

....

....

....

AMEN.

*Thank You, God,
for hearing my prayers!*

*Trust in the Lord with all your heart;
do not depend on your own understanding.*
PROVERBS 3:5

Date:

DEAR GOD, ...
....
....
....

I'm thankful for. . . ..
....
....
....
....
....
....
....
....
....

My worries. . .
....
....
....
....
....
....
....
....
....
....
....
....

People I am praying for. . .
....
....
....
....
....
....

Here's what's going on in my life. . . ..

....

....

....

....

....

....

My needs. . .

....

....

....

....

....

....

....

....

....

....

....

Other stuff I need to share with You, God. . .

....

....

....

....

....

....

....

AMEN.

Thank You, God, for hearing my prayers!

I prayed to the Lord, and he answered me. He freed me from all my fears.

PSALM 34:4

Date:

DEAR GOD, ...
....
....
....

I'm thankful for. . . ..
....
....
....
....
....
....
....
....

People I am praying for. . .
....
....
....
....
....
....

My worries. . .
....
....
....
....
....
....
....
....
....
....
....
....

Here's what's going on in my life. . . ..
....
....
....
....
....
....

My needs. . .
....
....
....
....
....
....
....
....
....
....
....

Other stuff I need to share with You, God. . .
....
....
....
....
....
....
....

AMEN.
Thank You, God, for hearing my prayers!

In every place of worship, I want men to pray with holy hands lifted up to God, free from anger and controversy.
1 TIMOTHY 2:8

Date:

DEAR GOD,

....
....
....
....

I'm thankful for. . . ..
....
....
....
....
....
....
....
....

People I am praying for. . .
....
....
....
....
....
....

My worries. . .
....
....
....
....
....
....
....
....
....
....
....
....
....
....

Here's what's going on in my life. . .

....
....
....
....
....
....

My needs. . .

....
....
....
....
....
....
....
....
....
....
....
....

Other stuff I need to share with You, God. . .

....
....
....
....
....

AMEN.

Thank You, God, for hearing my prayers!

"I tell you, you can pray for anything, and if you believe that you've received it, it will be yours."

MARK 11:24

Date:

DEAR GOD,

....
....
....
....

I'm thankful for. . . ..
....
....
....
....
....
....
....
....
....

My worries. . .
....
....
....
....
....
....
....
....
....
....
....
....
....

People I am praying for. . .
....
....
....
....
....
....

Here's what's going on in my life. . . ..

....

....

....

....

....

My needs. . .

....

....

....

....

....

....

....

....

....

....

....

Other stuff I need to share with You, God. . .

....

....

....

....

....

....

....

AMEN.

Thank You, God, for hearing my prayers!

Are any of you suffering hardships? You should pray. Are any of you happy? You should sing praises.

JAMES 5:13

Date:

DEAR GOD, ...
....
....
....

I'm thankful for. . . ..
....
....
....
....
....
....
....
....

People I am praying for. . .
....
....
....
....
....
....

My worries. . .
....
....
....
....
....
....
....
....
....
....
....
....
....

Here's what's going on in my life. . . ..
....
....
....
....
....
....

My needs. . .

....
....
....
....
....
....
....
....
....
....
....

Other stuff I need to share with You, God. . .

....
....
....
....
....
....
....
....

AMEN.

Thank You, God, for hearing my prayers!

I pray to you, O LORD. I say, "You are my place of refuge. You are all I really want in life."
PSALM 142:5

Date:

DEAR GOD, ...
....
....
....

I'm thankful for. . . ..
....
....
....
....
....
....
....
....

My worries. . .
....
....
....
....
....
....
....
....
....
....
....
....
....

People I am praying for. . .
....
....
....
....
....
....

Here's what's going on in my life. . . ..
....
....
....
....
....
....

My needs. . .
....
....
....
....
....
....
....
....
....
....
....
....

Other stuff I need to share with You, God. . .
....
....
....
....
....
....

AMEN.
Thank You, God, for hearing my prayers!

Remember that the heavenly Father to whom you pray has no favorites.
1 PETER 1:17

Date:

DEAR GOD,
....
....
....
....

I'm thankful for. . . ..
....
....
....
....
....
....
....
....
....

People I am praying for. . .
....
....
....
....
....
....

My worries. . .
....
....
....
....
....
....
....
....
....
....
....
....
....

Here's what's going on in my life... ....

....

....

....

....

....

....

My needs. . .

....

....

....

....

....

....

....

....

....

....

....

....

**Other stuff I need
to share with You, God. . .**

....

....

....

....

....

....

AMEN.

*Thank You, God,
for hearing my prayers!*

*If we are faithful to the end, trusting God
just as firmly as when we first believed,
we will share in all that belongs to Christ.*

HEBREWS 3:14

Date:

DEAR GOD, ...
....
....
....

I'm thankful for. . . ..
....
....
....
....
....
....
....
....

My worries. . .
....
....
....
....
....
....
....
....
....
....
....
....
....

People I am praying for. . .
....
....
....
....
....

Here's what's going on in my life. . .

....
....
....
....
....
....
....

My needs. . .

....
....
....
....
....
....
....
....
....
....
....
....

**Other stuff I need
to share with You, God. . .**

....
....
....
....
....
....
....

AMEN.
*Thank You, God,
for hearing my prayers!*

*The LORD. . .delights in the
prayers of the upright.*
PROVERBS 15:8

Date:

DEAR GOD, ...

....
....
....
....

I'm thankful for. . . ..

....
....
....
....
....
....
....
....

My worries. . .

....
....
....
....
....
....
....
....
....
....
....
....
....

People I am praying for. . .

....
....
....
....
....
....

Here's what's going on in my life. . .

....
....
....
....
....

My needs. . .

....
....
....
....
....
....
....
....
....
....
....
....

Other stuff I need to share with You, God. . .

....
....
....
....
....
....

AMEN.
Thank You, God, for hearing my prayers!

But you, dear friends, must build each other up in your most holy faith, pray in the power of the Holy Spirit.
JUDE 1:20

Date:

DEAR GOD,

....
....
....
....

I'm thankful for. . .
....
....
....
....
....
....
....
....
....

People I am praying for. . .
....
....
....
....
....

My worries. . .
....
....
....
....
....
....
....
....
....
....
....
....
....

Here's what's going on in my life. . .

My needs. . .

Other stuff I need to share with You, God. . .

AMEN.
Thank You, God, for hearing my prayers!

Bless those who persecute you. Don't curse them; pray that God will bless them.
ROMANS 12:14

Date: _____

DEAR GOD, ...
....
....
....

I'm thankful for. . . ..
....
....
....
....
....
....
....
....

People I am praying for. . .
....
....
....
....
....

My worries. . .
....
....
....
....
....
....
....
....
....
....
....
....
....

Here's what's going on in my life. . . ..
....
....
....
....
....
....

My needs. . .

....
....
....
....
....
....
....
....
....
....
....
....

**Other stuff I need
to share with You, God. . .**

....
....
....
....
....
....
....
....

AMEN.

*Thank You, God,
for hearing my prayers!*

The Lord will answer my prayer.
PSALM 6:9

Date:

DEAR GOD, ...
....
....
....

I'm thankful for. . . ..
....
....
....
....
....
....
....
....

People I am praying for. . .
....
....
....
....
....

My worries. . .
....
....
....
....
....
....
....
....
....
....
....
....

Here's what's going on in my life. . .

....

....

....

....

....

....

My needs. . .

....

....

....

....

....

....

....

....

....

....

....

**Other stuff I need
to share with You, God. . .**

....

....

....

....

....

....

AMEN.

*Thank You, God,
for hearing my prayers!*

God can be trusted to keep his promise.

HEBREWS 10:23

Date:

DEAR GOD, ...
....
....
....

I'm thankful for. . . ..
....
....
....
....
....
....
....
....

My worries. . .
....
....
....
....
....
....
....
....
....
....
....
....
....
....

People I am praying for. . .
....
....
....
....
....

Here's what's going on in my life. . . ..

....

....

....

....

....

....

My needs. . .

....

....

....

....

....

....

....

....

....

....

....

**Other stuff I need
to share with You, God. . .**

....

....

....

....

....

....

AMEN.

*Thank You, God,
for hearing my prayers!*

*But I'm in the very presence of God—
oh, how refreshing it is!*

PSALM 73:27 MSG

Date: _____

DEAR GOD, ...
....
....
....

I'm thankful for... ....
....
....
....
....
....
....
....
....
....

My worries. . .
....
....
....
....
....
....
....
....
....
....
....
....
....
....

People I am praying for. . .
....
....
....
....
....

Here's what's going on in my life. . .

....

....

....

....

....

....

My needs. . .

....

....

....

....

....

....

....

....

....

....

....

**Other stuff I need
to share with You, God. . .**

....

....

....

....

....

....

....

AMEN.

*Thank You, God,
for hearing my prayers!*

*Let your unfailing love surround us,
Lord, for our hope is in you alone.*
PSALM 33:22

Date:

DEAR GOD,

....
....
....
....

I'm thankful for. . .

....
....
....
....
....
....
....
....
....
....

People I am praying for. . .

....
....
....
....
....

My worries. . .

....
....
....
....
....
....
....
....
....
....
....
....
....
....

Here's what's going on in my life. . . ..
....
....
....
....
....
....

My needs. . .
....
....
....
....
....
....
....
....
....
....
....
....

Other stuff I need to share with You, God. . .

....
....
....
....
....
....
....

AMEN.
Thank You, God, for hearing my prayers!

Pray. . .for kings and all who are in authority so that we can live peaceful and quiet lives marked by godliness and dignity.
1 TIMOTHY 2:2

Date:

DEAR GOD, ...
....
....
....

I'm thankful for. . . ..
....
....
....
....
....
....
....
....
....

My worries. . .
....
....
....
....
....
....
....
....
....
....
....
....
....

People I am praying for. . .
....
....
....
....
....

Here's what's going on in my life. . .

....

....

....

....

....

....

My needs. . .

....

....

....

....

....

....

....

....

....

....

....

Other stuff I need to share with You, God. . .

....

....

....

....

....

....

....

AMEN.

Thank You, God, for hearing my prayers!

O Lord, you alone are my hope.

PSALM 71:5

Date:

DEAR GOD, ...
....
....
....

I'm thankful for. . . ..
....
....
....
....
....
....
....
....

People I am praying for. . .
....
....
....
....
....
....

My worries. . .
....
....
....
....
....
....
....
....
....
....
....
....
....

Here's what's going on in my life. . . ..

....

....

....

....

....

My needs. . .

....

....

....

....

....

....

....

....

....

....

....

....

**Other stuff I need
to share with You, God. . .**

....

....

....

....

....

....

AMEN.

*Thank You, God,
for hearing my prayers!*

*"The eyes of the LORD watch over
those who do right, and his ears
are open to their prayers."*
1 PETER 3:12

Date:

DEAR GOD, ...
....
....
....

I'm thankful for. . . ..
....
....
....
....
....
....
....
....

My worries. . .
....
....
....
....
....
....
....
....
....
....
....
....
....

People I am praying for. . .
....
....
....
....
....

Here's what's going on in my life. . . ..
....
....
....
....
....
....

My needs. . .

....
....
....
....
....
....
....
....
....
....
....
....

**Other stuff I need
to share with You, God. . .**

....
....
....
....
....
....
....

AMEN.

*Thank You, God,
for hearing my prayers!*

*"But when you pray, go away by yourself,
shut the door behind you, and pray to
your Father in private. Then your Father,
who sees everything, will reward you."*

MATTHEW 6:6

Date:

DEAR GOD,
....
....
....
....

I'm thankful for. . . ..
....
....
....
....
....
....
....
....

People I am praying for. . .
....
....
....
....
....
....

My worries. . .
....
....
....
....
....
....
....
....
....
....
....
....
....
....

Here's what's going on in my life. . .
....
....
....
....
....
....

My needs. . .
....
....
....
....
....
....
....
....
....
....
....
....

**Other stuff I need
to share with You, God. . .**

AMEN.
*Thank You, God,
for hearing my prayers!*

Be earnest and disciplined in your prayers.
1 PETER 4:7

Date:

DEAR GOD,

....
....
....
....

I'm thankful for. . .

....
....
....
....
....
....
....
....

People I am praying for. . .

....
....
....
....
....

My worries. . .

....
....
....
....
....
....
....
....
....
....
....
....
....

Here's what's going on in my life. . . ..
....
....
....
....
....
....

My needs. . .

....
....
....
....
....
....
....
....
....
....
....
....

**Other stuff I need
to share with You, God. . .**

....
....
....
....
....
....
....
....

AMEN.

*Thank You, God,
for hearing my prayers!*

*Hallelujah! O my soul, praise GOD!
All my life long I'll praise GOD, singing
songs to my God as long as I live.*
PSALM 146:1–2 MSG

Date:

DEAR GOD,

....
....
....
....

I'm thankful for. . .

....
....
....
....
....
....
....
....
....

People I am praying for. . .

....
....
....
....
....

My worries. . .

....
....
....
....
....
....
....
....
....
....
....
....
....
....

Here's what's going on in my life. . .

....

....

....

....

....

My needs. . .

....

....

....

....

....

....

....

....

....

....

....

Other stuff I need to share with You, God. . .

AMEN.

Thank You, God, for hearing my prayers!

When doubts filled my mind, your comfort gave me renewed hope and cheer.

PSALM 94:19

Date:

DEAR GOD, ...
....
....
....

I'm thankful for. . . ..
....
....
....
....
....
....
....
....
....

My worries. . .
....
....
....
....
....
....
....
....
....
....
....
....
....

People I am praying for. . .
....
....
....
....
....

Here's what's going on in my life. . .

....
....
....
....
....
....

My needs. . .

....
....
....
....
....
....
....
....
....
....
....
....

**Other stuff I need
to share with You, God. . .**

....
....
....
....
....

AMEN.

*Thank You, God,
for hearing my prayers!*

*I am counting on the LORD;
yes, I am counting on him.*
PSALM 130:5

Date:

DEAR GOD,

....
....
....
....

I'm thankful for. . .
....
....
....
....
....
....
....
....
....

People I am praying for. . .
....
....
....
....
....
....

My worries. . .
....
....
....
....
....
....
....
....
....
....
....
....
....
....

Here's what's going on in my life. . .

....
....
....
....
....
....

My needs. . .

....
....
....
....
....
....
....
....
....
....
....
....

Other stuff I need to share with You, God. . .

....
....
....
....
....
....

AMEN.

Thank You, God, for hearing my prayers!

*"No one who trusts God like this—
heart and soul—will ever regret it."*

ROMANS 10:11 MSG

Date:

DEAR GOD,

....
....
....
....

I'm thankful for. . . ..
....
....
....
....
....
....
....
....

People I am praying for. . .
....
....
....
....
....

My worries. . .

....
....
....
....
....
....
....
....
....
....
....
....

Here's what's going on in my life. . .

....
....
....
....
....
....

My needs. . .

....
....
....
....
....
....
....
....
....
....
....

Other stuff I need to share with You, God. . .

....
....
....
....
....
....

AMEN.
Thank You, God, for hearing my prayers!

The hopes of the godly result in happiness.
PROVERBS 10:28

Date:

DEAR GOD,

....
....
....
....

I'm thankful for. . . ..

....
....
....
....
....
....
....
....

My worries. . .
....
....
....
....
....
....
....
....
....
....
....
....
....

People I am praying for. . .

....
....
....
....
....
....

Here's what's going on in my life. . . ..
....
....
....
....
....
....

My needs. . .
....
....
....
....
....
....
....
....
....
....
....
....

**Other stuff I need
to share with You, God. . .**
....
....
....
....
....
....
....

AMEN.
*Thank You, God,
for hearing my prayers!*

*God knows how often I pray for you. Day and
night I bring you and your needs in prayer
to God, whom I serve with all my heart by
spreading the Good News about his Son.*

ROMANS 1:9

Date:

DEAR GOD, ...
....
....
....

I'm thankful for. . . ..
....
....
....
....
....
....
....
....

My worries. . .
....
....
....
....
....
....
....
....
....
....
....
....
....

People I am praying for. . .
....
....
....
....
....

Here's what's going on in my life. . . ..
....
....
....
....
....

My needs. . .
....
....
....
....
....
....
....
....
....
....
....

**Other stuff I need
to share with You, God. . .**

....
....
....
....
....
....

AMEN.
*Thank You, God,
for hearing my prayers!*

*You're my place of quiet retreat;
I wait for your Word to renew me.*
PSALM 119:114 MSG

Date:

DEAR GOD, ...
....
....
....

I'm thankful for. . . ..
....
....
....
....
....
....
....
....

People I am praying for. . .
....
....
....
....
....

My worries. . .
....
....
....
....
....
....
....
....
....
....
....
....
....
....

Here's what's going on in my life. . .

....

....

....

....

....

My needs. . .

....

....

....

....

....

....

....

....

....

....

....

Other stuff I need to share with You, God. . .

....

....

....

....

....

....

....

AMEN.

Thank You, God, for hearing my prayers!

Quiet down before GOD, be prayerful before him.
PSALM 37:7 MSG

Date:

DEAR GOD, ...
....
....
....

I'm thankful for. . . ..
....
....
....
....
....
....
....
....

People I am praying for. . .
....
....
....
....
....

My worries. . .
....
....
....
....
....
....
....
....
....
....
....
....
....
....

Here's what's going on in my life. . .

....
....
....
....
....
....

My needs. . .

....
....
....
....
....
....
....
....
....
....
....
....

**Other stuff I need
to share with You, God. . .**

....
....
....
....
....
....
....

AMEN.

*Thank You, God,
for hearing my prayers!*

*I thank you for answering my
prayer and giving me victory!*
PSALM 118:21

Date:

DEAR GOD, ...
....
....
....

I'm thankful for. . . ..
....
....
....
....
....
....
....

People I am praying for. . .
....
....
....
....

My worries. . .
....
....
....
....
....
....
....
....
....
....
....
....
....

Here's what's going on in my life. . . ..

....

....

....

....

....

....

My needs. . .

....

....

....

....

....

....

....

....

....

....

....

....

**Other stuff I need
to share with You, God. . .**

....

....

....

....

....

....

AMEN.

*Thank You, God,
for hearing my prayers!*

*I pray that your hearts will be flooded with
light so that you can understand the confident
hope he has given to those he called.*

EPHESIANS 1:18

Date:

DEAR GOD,

....
....
....
....

I'm thankful for. . . ..
....
....
....
....
....
....
....
....
....

People I am praying for. . .
....
....
....
....
....
....

My worries. . .

....
....
....
....
....
....
....
....
....
....
....
....
....
....

Here's what's going on in my life. . .

....
....
....
....
....
....

My needs. . .

....
....
....
....
....
....
....
....
....
....
....
....

Other stuff I need to share with You, God. . .

....
....
....
....
....
....

AMEN.

Thank You, God, for hearing my prayers!

Answer me when I call to you, O God.

PSALM 4:1

Date:

DEAR GOD, ...
....
....
....

I'm thankful for. . . ..
....
....
....
....
....
....
....
....
....

People I am praying for. . .
....
....
....
....
....

My worries. . .
....
....
....
....
....
....
....
....
....
....
....
....
....

Here's what's going on in my life. . . . .

. . . .

. . . .

. . . .

. . . .

. . . .

My needs. . .

. . . .

. . . .

. . . .

. . . .

. . . .

. . . .

. . . .

. . . .

. . . .

. . . .

. . . .

. . . .

Other stuff I need to share with You, God. . .

. . . .

. . . .

. . . .

. . . .

. . . .

. . . .

. . . .

AMEN.
*Thank You, God,
for hearing my prayers!*

*Every time I think of you,
I give thanks to my God.*
PHILIPPIANS 1:3

Date:

DEAR GOD, ...
....
....
....

I'm thankful for. . . ..
....
....
....
....
....
....
....
....

People I am praying for. . .
....
....
....
....

My worries. . .
....
....
....
....
....
....
....
....
....
....
....
....
....

Here's what's going on in my life. . .

....

....

....

....

....

....

My needs. . .

....

....

....

....

....

....

....

....

....

....

....

....

Other stuff I need to share with You, God. . .

....

....

....

....

....

....

....

AMEN.
Thank You, God,
for hearing my prayers!

Never stop praying.
1 THESSALONIANS 5:17

MORE ENCOURAGEMENT FOR YOUR BEAUTIFUL SPIRIT!

You Belong:
Devotions and Prayers for a Teen Girl's Heart

You Were Created with Purpose by a Loving, Heavenly Creator. . .*You Belong*!

This delightful devotional is a lovely reminder that you were created with purpose by a heavenly Creator. . .and that you belong—right here and now—in this world. One hundred eighty encouraging readings and inspiring prayers, rooted in biblical truth, will reassure your uncertain heart, helping you to understand that you're *never* alone and *always* loved. In each devotional reading, you will encounter the bountiful blessings and grace of your Creator, while coming to trust His purposeful plan for you in this world.

Flexible Casebound / 978-1-63609-169-3